STORNOWAY PRIMARY SCHOOL
JAMIESON DRIVE
STORNOWAY

KT-161-918

STORNOWAY
JAMES
STO.....TE

Friends

Nicola Baxter

Watts Books
London ● New York ● Sydney

Everyone needs friends.

A friend can be someone who is like you or someone with memories to share.

2

3

A friend is someone you feel happy with.
You like doing the same things together.
Maybe you agree about what
you don't like too!

What do you like to do with your friends?

Try this later
Draw a picture of you and your best friend,
whoever it might be.

A real friend helps you with a problem. It's easier to sort things out with someone else.

Can you remember a time when a friend helped you out?

Friends talk things over.
A good friend can keep a special secret.

Friends can have quiet times together, too.

Friends are always pleased to see you. Sometimes they have a special way of showing how they feel.

How do your friends know that
you are happy to see them?

Friends remember when it is your birthday.

How do you make sure you remember your friends' birthdays?

Try this later

Make a special ... to give to a friend.

Sometimes friends get angry
with each other.

But they soon make up and
are friends again.

Some people seem to have
lots of friends.
Some people like to have
one special friend.

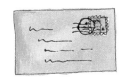

Sometimes friends live far apart.
But they can still talk to each other or
send special messages.

 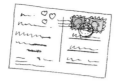   

Try this later

There are lots of ways to keep in touch.
Try making a tape-recording to tell
someone all about the things you do.

Friends like to share their favourite things.

They take turns and try to be fair.

Friends have fun together!

23

Index

© 1996 Watts Books

Watts Books
96 Leonard Street
London EC2A 4RH

Franklin Watts Australia
14 Mars Road
Lane Cove NSW 2066

ISBN: 0 7496 2174 5

Dewey Decimal Classification
Number 302.3

A CIP catalogue record for this
book is available from the British
Library.

1 2 3 4 5 6 7 8 9 10

Editor: Sarah Ridley
Designer: Nina Kingsbury
Illustrator: Michael Evans

The publishers would like to thank
Carol Olivier, Osbert Clements
and Liane Bates of Kenmont

Primary School for their help with
the cover of this book.

Photographs: Bubbles 4, 9, 12, 18,
20; Robert Harding Picture Library
10; Peter Millard cover; Trip 17;
ZEFA 3, 15.

Printed in Malaysia